Tu Es Diaboli Ianua

Christianity, The Johannine Weltanschauung, And Presencing The Numinous

David Myatt

○○○

Contents

Exordium

Given that the religion termed Christianity has, for over six centuries, been influential in respect of the ethos and spirituality of the culture of the West - often to the extent of having been described as manifesting that ethos and that spirituality - one of the metaphysical questions I have saught to answer over the past forty years is whether that religion is, given our thousands of years old human culture of pathei-mathos, a suitable presencing of the numinous. If it is not, then could that religion be reformed, by developing a Johannine Weltanschauung given that the Gospel According to John - τὸ κατὰ Ἰωάννην εὐαγγέλιον - arguably presents a somewhat different perspective on the life and teachings of Jesus of Nazareth than the three other synoptic Gospels. Would such a reformation be a suitable presencing of the numinous, and if not, then what non-Christian alternatives - such as a paganus metaphysics - exist, and what is the foundation of such an alternative?

This essay presents my answers to such questions and thus compliments my book *Classical Paganism And The Christian Ethos*. As in that book, I have made extensive use of my translations of certain classical authors and of various hermetic texts as well as the Gospel of John, and given that those translations are currently quite accessible I have not except on a few occasions explained my interpretations of certain Greek or Latin terms since those interpretations are explained in the associated commentaries.

As noted elsewhere, I prefer the term paganus - a transliteration of the classical Latin, denoting as it does connection to Nature, to the natural, more rural, world - in preference to 'pagan' since paganus is, in my view and in respect of the Greco-Roman ethos, more accurate given what the term 'pagan' now often denotes.

The title of the essay, Tu Es Diaboli Ianua - "You Are The Nexion Of The Deofel", literally, "You are nexion Diabolos " - is taken from Tertullian's *De Monogamia*, written at the beginning of the second century AD.

David Myatt
Winter Solstice 2017

∘∘∘

I. The Johannine Weltanschauung And The Numinous

The Numinous

The religion [1] of Christianity is founded on, and regarded as being manifest in, the Greek texts that have become known as the Canonical New Testament, Καινὴ Διαθήκη, and the Greek texts known as the Septuagint (LXX, The Old Testament) with such texts being regarded as divinely inspired and thus, in the words of Tertullian, Divinum Instrumentum, [2] [3] the divine apparatus - the instrument - for understanding divine decree.

Writing in the early years of the Christian religion, Tertullian expressed the essence of the Christian ethos when he wrote:

> Post vetera exempla originalium personarum aeque ad vetera transeamus instrumenta legalium scripturarum [...] quam Christus non dissolvit, sed adimplevit. [4]

> Given the venerable examples of the ancient ones, consider the venerable apparatus of scriptural Law [...] which Christ did not nullify, but fulfilled.

Which reliance on such written words from 'the ancient ones' (the Prophets) and from the authors of the New Testament, and which understanding of those words as divinely inspired and thus as the definitive guide to what is sacred and what is profane, led not only to views such as the following but also to such views becoming a part of the Christian ethos and a part of Christian praxis for well over a thousand years:

> Viuit sententia Dei super sexum istum in hoc saeculo: uiuat et reatus necesse est. Tu es diaboli ianua; tu es arboris illius resignatrix; tu es diuinae legis prima desertrix; tu es quae eum suasisti, quem diabolus aggredi non ualuit; tu imaginem Dei, hominem, tam facile elisisti; propter tuum meritum, id est mortem, etiam filius Dei mori habuit. [5]

> The judgement of God on your gender is alive in this era, necessitating that you live with your offence. You are The Nexion of The Deofel. You are The Resignatrix of The Tree. You are The Archetypal Desertrix of Divine Decree. You are she who incited he

whom The Deofel could not attack. You effortlessly broke the representation of God: a man. And it is because of you - because of your loss - that even the Son of God had to die. [6]

Which rather harsh indictment of half of humanity, with its accusations, its sternness, and its apparent lack of empathy, inclines one to enquire into the nature of the numinous and thus into how we, as individuals and sans preconceptions, can distinguish the 'sacred' from the 'profane'.

My, admittedly fallible, understanding of the numinous is that it is a presencing, and an apprehension by us, of the divine, of the sacred. Which apprehension is of our physis [7] as human beings, and thus of our relation to other human beings, to other living beings, and to the Cosmos itself. An apprehension - a perceiveration - that enables a supra-personal 'cosmic' perspective and which perspective can incline us as individuals toward humility and thus comprehend our mortality and our fallible nature. In effect, this apprehension is the genesis of mysticism since it is a personal intuitive insight about the nature of Reality where there is a wordless - and empathic, a contemplative - apprehension of there existing certain truths which transcend the temporal, the causal, and thus which are beyond the denotatum of words, categories, dogma, ideology, and thus beyond named ideas.

The Johannine Weltanschauung

Would a Christianity based only on the Gospel According to John - τὸ κατὰ Ἰωάννην εὐαγγέλιον - be different from, more numinous than, the Christianity derived from the Gospels of Matthew, Mark, and Luke, and the other texts included in what has become known as the Canonical New Testament, Καινὴ Διαθήκη? A Johannine Christianity where the Greek texts known as LXX, the Old Testament, were not regarded as 'the Word of God' - as divinely inspired and canonical - but rather as providing some historical background to the old, superseded, logos of Mosaic law and of 'the Prophets'. Would such a Johannine Christianity be a Weltanschauung - a particular and individual apprehension or interpretation of Reality - rather than a religion with all that a religion implies in terms of hierarchy and dogma? With the contrast being, in the words of Tertullian, Post vetera exempla originalium personarum aeque ad vetera transeamus instrumenta legalium scripturarum.

What emerges from my reading of τὸ κατὰ Ἰωάννην εὐαγγέλιον [8] is rather reminiscent of what individuals such as Julian of Norwich, George Fox, and William Penn wrote and said about Jesus and the spiritual way that the Gospels in particular revealed. This is the way of humility, of forgiveness, of love, of a personal appreciation of the divine, of the numinous; and a spiritual, interior, way somewhat different from supra-personal moralistic interpretations based on inflexible notions of 'sin' and thus on what is or has doctrinally been considered 'good' and what is considered 'evil'.

A difference evident in many passages from the Gospel of John, such as the following two, one of which involves the Greek word πιστεύω, and which word is perhaps a relevant hermeneutical example. The conventional interpretation of meaning, in respect of New Testament texts, is 'believe', 'have faith in', so that John 3:16 is interpreted along the following lines:

> For God so loved the world, that he gave his only begotten Son, that whosoever believeth in him should not perish, but have everlasting life. (King James Bible)

Similarly in respect of other verses where πιστεύω occurs, so that the impression is of the necessity of believing, of having or acquiring faith.

Yet, and in regard to the aforementioned verse, if one interprets that particular (and another) Greek word in a more Hellenistic – a more Greek – way, then one has:

> Theos so loved the world that he offered up his only begotten son so that all those trusting in him would not perish but might have life everlasting.

Not only is this personal, direct – as in personally trusting someone as opposed to a 'blind believing' – but there are no prior hermeneutic assumptions about 'God', derived as such assumptions are from over two thousand years of scriptural exegesis and preaching.

Example One. Chapter Three, 16-21

DWM:

> Theos so loved the world that he offered up his only begotten son so that all those trusting in him would not perish but might have life everlasting. For Theos did not dispatch his son to the world to condemn the world, but rather that the world might be rescued through him. Whosoever trusts in him is not condemned while whomsoever does not trust is condemned for he has not trusted in the Nomen of the only begotten son of Theos.
>
> And this is the condemnation: That the Phaos arrived in the world but mortals loved the darkness more than the Phaos, for their deeds were harmful. For anyone who does what is mean dislikes the Phaos and does not come near the Phaos lest their deeds be exposed. But whomsoever practices disclosure goes to the Phaos so that their deeds might be manifest as having been done through Theos. [9]

King James Bible:

God so loved the world, that he gave his only begotten Son, that whosoever believeth in him should not perish, but have everlasting life. For God sent not his Son into the world to condemn the world; but that the world through him might be saved. He that believeth on him is not condemned: but he that believeth not is condemned already, because he hath not believed in the name of the only begotten Son of God. And this is the condemnation, that light is come into the world, and men loved darkness rather than light, because their deeds were evil. For every one that doeth evil hateth the light, neither cometh to the light, lest his deeds should be reproved. But he that doeth truth cometh to the light, that his deeds may be made manifest, that they are wrought in God.

Example Two. Chapter Five, 1-16

DWM:

Following this, there was a Judaean feast and Jesus went to Jerusalem. And there is in Jerusalem by the place of the sheep a pool, named in the language of the Hebrews as Bethesda, which has five colonnades in which were a large number of the infirm – the blind, the limping, the withered – awaiting a change in the water since on occasion an Envoy of Theos descended into the pool, stirring the water, and whomsoever after that stirring of the water was first to enter became complete, the burden of their affliction removed.

And there was a man there who for eight and thirty years had been infirm. Jesus, seeing him lying there and knowing of that lengthy duration, said to him: "Do you seek to be complete?"

The infirm one replied: "Sir, I do not have someone who when the water is stirred could place me in that pool, and, when I go, someone else has descended before me."

Jesus said to him: "Arise. Take your bedroll, and walk."

And, directly, the man became complete, took up his bedroll and walked around. And it was the day of the Sabbath.

Thus did the Judaeans say to the one who had been treated: "It is the Sabbath and it is not permitted for you to carry your bedroll."

To them he answered: "It was he who made me complete who said for me to take my bedroll and to walk around."

So they asked him: "Who is the man who said for you to take the bedroll and walk?"

But the healed one did not know, for there was a crowd there with Jesus having betaken himself away.

Following this, Jesus discovered him in the temple and said to him: "Behold, you are complete. No more missteps, lest something worse befalls you."

The man then went away and informed the Judaeans that it was Jesus who had made him complete, and thus did the Judaeans harass Jesus because he was doing such things on the Sabbath. [10][11]

King James Bible:

After this there was a feast of the Jews; and Jesus went up to Jerusalem.

Now there is at Jerusalem by the sheep market a pool, which is called in the Hebrew tongue Bethesda, having five porches. In these lay a great multitude of impotent folk, of blind, halt, withered, waiting for the moving of the water. For an angel went down at a certain season into the pool, and troubled the water: whosoever then first after the troubling of the water stepped in was made whole of whatsoever disease he had. And a certain man was there, which had an infirmity thirty and eight years. When Jesus saw him lie, and knew that he had been now a long time in that case, he saith unto him, Wilt thou be made whole? The impotent man answered him, Sir, I have no man, when the water is troubled, to put me into the pool: but while I am coming, another steppeth down before me. Jesus saith unto him, Rise, take up thy bed, and walk. And immediately the man was made whole, and took up his bed, and walked: and on the same day was the sabbath.

The Jews therefore said unto him that was cured, It is the sabbath day: it is not lawful for thee to carry thy bed. He answered them, He that made me whole, the same said unto me, Take up thy bed, and walk. Then asked they him, What man is that which said unto thee, Take up thy bed, and walk? And he that was healed wist not who it was: for Jesus had conveyed himself away, a multitude being in that place. Afterward Jesus findeth him in the temple, and said unto him, Behold, thou art made whole: sin no more, lest a worse thing come unto thee. The man departed, and told the Jews that it was Jesus, which had made him whole.

And therefore did the Jews persecute Jesus, and sought to slay him, because he had done these things on the sabbath day.

Summary

The first example seems to me to be revealing of the personal nature of the 'way of Jesus of Nazareth' – of a personal trust in a particular person, in this instance a trust in Jesus because of how he and his life are recounted by the Evangelist – contrasting with a rather impersonal demand to believe, to have faith, based on doctrine as codified by someone else or by some organized regulatory and supra-local hierarchy.

The second example seems to me to be revealing of the contrast between the then organized supra-personal religion of the Judaeans – with its doctrinal forbiddance, sometimes on pain of death, of certain personal deeds – and the empathy and compassion of an individual, as evident in Jesus in the immediacy of the moment healing a long-suffering infirm man and bidding him to take up and carry his bedroll, undoubtedly aware as Jesus was that he was doing and inciting what was forbidden because for him empathy and compassion were more important than some established doctrine.

Is this contrast between what seems to be a particular dogmatism, a particular religious (hubriatic) intolerance by the Judaeans, and an individual being empathic and compassionate in the immediacy of the moment, still relevant today? Personally, I do believe it is, leading me to conclude that τὸ κατὰ Ἰωάννην εὐαγγέλιον – The Gospel According To John – contains certain truths not only about our physis as human beings but also about our relation to Being, to the divine, to the numinous. For, as described in tractate III of the Corpus Hermeticum,

> Δόξα πάντων ὁ θεὸς καὶ θεῖον καὶ φύσις θεία. ἀρχὴ τῶν ὄντων ὁ θεός, καὶ νοῦς καὶ φύσις καὶ ὕλη, σοφία εἰς δεῖξιν ἁπάντων ὤν· ἀρχὴ τὸ θεῖον καὶ φύσις καὶ ἐνέργεια καὶ ἀνάγκη καὶ τέλος καὶ ἀνανέωσις [...] τὸ γὰρ θεῖον ἡ πᾶσα κοσμικὴ σύγκρασις φύσει ἀνανεουμένη· ἐν γὰρ τῶι θείωι καὶ ἡ φύσις καθέστηκεν.

> The numen of all beings is theos: numinal, and of numinal physis. The origin of what exists is theos, who is Perceiveration and Physis and Substance: the sapientia which is a revealing of all beings. For the numinal is the origin: physis, vigour, incumbency, accomplishment, renewance [...]

> The divine is all of that mixion: renewance of the cosmic order through Physis, for Physis is presenced in the divine. [12]

∘∘∘

II. A Paganus Apprehension

The particular truths revealed by the Gospel of John - that is, of a more personal way to apprehend the divine through an individual trust in a particular living person, the person of Jesus - are however dependant on three things. First, on accepting the veracity of a particular written text. Second, on an acceptance that certain signs (σημεῖᾶ) - such as the Passion, the death and resurrection of Jesus, and his Ascension - indicate that he is, as the Evangelist narrates, the Son of Theos and thus can gift mortals with life everlasting. Third, that the person in question - Jesus - is alive and thus could be personally known and trusted on the basis of such a personal knowing.

If one accepts that the narration is a reasonably accurate portrayal of the life of a particular individual then one might be inclined to appreciate that Jesus - judged by our thousands of years old human culture of pathei-mathos [13] - presenced a certain wisdom, a certain understanding of the divine and of our human physis, manifest for example in compassion and in eschewing contemporary religious restrictions dogmatically imposed upon individuals.

Yet for we who live centuries after the narrated death of Jesus to extend this appreciation of a once living mortal to an acceptance of him as the Son of God, able thus to gift us with life everlasting because he is not a mere mortal, not dead, but rather a living, a resurrected, an immortal divinity, is not an act of trust based on a personal knowing of a living mortal but rather is an act of faith, a spiritual act of belief.

Thus a Christianity based only on the Gospel According to John would not, in its essence and in my fallible opinion, be very different from the Christianity derived from the Canonical New Testament, since the Gospel According to John would become Divinum Instrumentum, the divine apparatus for understanding divine decree - and become so regardless of whether or not such an apparatus included The Old Testament - with the attendant development of dogma and exegesis and thence the subsequent schisms based on the various interpretations suggested by such exegesis.

For the problem is - or so it seems to me - in impersonal written texts. Or, more precisely, in denotatum, and thus in assigning terms - in using words - to describe an apprehension of the numinous. Which leads us to the fundamental difference between a religious apprehension of the numinous - based on received and venerated texts, on exegesis - and the paganus apprehension of the numinous as manifest in Greco-Roman culture, based as it is on an individual, and an intuitive, empathic and thus wordless, apprehension of the numinous. Which paganism will be examined for two reasons. Firstly, because it is manifest in a multiplicity of primary sources - from Homer to Hesiod to Cicero and beyond - and secondly because Greco-Roman culture is inextricably bound to the culture of the West and formed the basis for the European Renaissance that emerged in the 14th century, one aspect of which was a widespread appreciation of classical Art, of classical literature, and of texts such as the Corpus Hermeticum.

The Greco-Roman paganus apprehension is presenced for us in mythoi - myths and legends - none of which were regarded as embodying a religious revelation from an omnipotent deity to his 'chosen people' and none of which embodied divine commands - divine laws - which mortals were commanded to obey on pain of punishment. Instead, these myths and legends - described by Homer, by Hesiod, and dramatised by Aeschylus, Sophocles, and others - were instructive examples of how the gods interacted with other divinities and with mortals, and how mortals should interact among themselves and with the gods.

Thus in Greek mythoi the divine chieftain, Zeus, in an instructive example of the ancient Greek principle of δημοκρατία, is depicted by Homer in Book I, vv. 76-77 of The Odyssey as saying to the goddess Athena that there will a gathering of the gods in order to discuss and consider the matter of the return of Odysseus to his home, ἀλλ᾽ ἄγεθ᾽ ἡμεῖς οἵδε περιφραζώμεθα πάντες νόστον.

Which mention of Athena illustrates two of the many fundamental differences between classical paganism and the monotheism of Christianity accepting as that monotheism does the beliefs of the ancient Hebrews as mentioned in the Gospel of John and as described in the Old Testament. A first difference is how some deities - such as Pallas Athena - would shapeshift and assume various forms, including human form, in order to directly interact with mortals, with the goddess Athena in the Odyssey assuming the form of a mortal man. A second difference is a polytheism which includes many female deities, with such female deities often considered by mortals as friends and companions and invoked for assistance, a personal, an intimate, apprehension beautifully expressed by Sappho:

> Ποικιλόθρον᾽ ἀθάνατ᾽ Ἀφροδιτα,
> παῖ Δίοσ, δολόπλοκε, λίσσομαί σε
> μή μ᾽ ἄσαισι μήτ᾽ ὀνίαισι δάμνα,
> πότνια, θῦμον
>
> ἀλλά τυίδ᾽ ἔλθ᾽, αἴποτα κἀτέρωτα
> τᾶσ ἔμασ αὔδωσ αΐοισα πήλγι
> ἔκλυεσ πάτροσ δὲ δόμον λίποισα
> χρύσιον ἦλθεσ
>
> ἄρμ᾽ ὑποζεύξαια, κάλοι δέ σ᾽ ἄγον

ὤκεεσ στροῦθοι περὶ γᾶσ μελαίνασ
πύκνα δινεῦντεσ πτέρ ἀπ᾽ ὠράνω
αἴθεροσ διὰ μέσσω

αῖψα δ᾽ ἐχίκοντο, σὺ δ᾽, ὦ μάσαιρα
μειδιάσαισ᾽ ἀθάνατῳ προσώπῳ,
ἤρέ ὄττι δηῦτε πέπονθα κὤττι
δἤγτε κάλημι

κὤττι μοι μάλιστα θέλω γένεσθαι
μαινόλᾳ θύμῳ, τίνα δηῦτε πείθω
μαῖσ ἄγην ἐσ σὰν φιλότατα τίσ τ, ὦ
Πσάπφ᾽, ἀδίκηει

καὶ γάρ αἰ φεύγει, ταχέωσ διώξει,
αἰ δὲ δῶρα μὴ δέκετ ἀλλά δώσει,
αἰ δὲ μὴ φίλει ταχέωσ φιλήσει,
κωὐκ ἐθέλοισα

ἔλθε μοι καὶ νῦν, χαλεπᾶν δὲ λῦσον
ἐκ μερίμναν ὄσσα δέ μοι τέλεσσαι
θῦμοσ ἰμμέρρει τέλεσον, σὺ δ᾽ αὖτα
σύμμαχοσ ἔσσο.

Deathless Aphrodite – Daughter of Zeus and maker of snares -
On your florid throne, hear me!
My lady, do not subdue my heart by anguish and pain
But come to me as when before
You heard my distant cry, and listened:
Leaving, with your golden chariot yoked, your father's house
To move beautiful sparrows swift with a whirling of wings
As from heaven you came to this dark earth through middle air
And so swiftly arrived.

Then you my goddess with your immortal lips smiling
Would ask what now afflicts me, why again
I am calling and what now I with my restive heart
Desired:

Whom now shall I beguile
To bring you to her love?
Who now injures you, Sappho?
For if she flees, soon shall she chase
And, rejecting gifts, soon shall she give.
If she does not love you, she shall do so soon
Whatsoever is her will.

Come to me now to end this consuming pain
Bringing what my heart desires to be brought:
Be yourself my ally in this fight.

Female deities could, like Athena, intervene in the life of mortals and so alter their fate even to the extent of guiding them toward their death. For it is not Zeus alone who - as a monotheistic omnipotent deity does - decides the fate of mortals, but also other gods, as described for instance by Homer:

ἄνδρα μοι ἔννεπε, μοῦσα, πολύτροπον, ὃς μάλα πολλὰ
πλάγχθη, ἐπεὶ Τροίης ἱερὸν πτολίεθρον ἔπερσεν:
πολλῶν δ᾽ ἀνθρώπων ἴδεν ἄστεα καὶ νόον ἔγνω,
πολλὰ δ᾽ ὅ γ᾽ ἐν πόντῳ πάθεν ἄλγεα ὃν κατὰ θυμόν,
ἀρνύμενος ἥν τε ψυχὴν καὶ νόστον ἑταίρων.
ἀλλ᾽ οὐδ᾽ ὣς ἑτάρους ἐρρύσατο, ἱέμενός περ:
αὐτῶν γὰρ σφετέρῃσιν ἀτασθαλίῃσιν ὄλοντο,
νήπιοι, οἳ κατὰ βοῦς Ὑπερίονος Ἠελίοιο
ἤσθιον: αὐτὰρ ὁ τοῖσιν ἀφείλετο νόστιμον ἦμαρ

The Muse shall tell of the many adventures of that man of the many stratagems
Who, after the pillage of that hallowed citadel at Troy,
Saw the towns of many a people and experienced their ways:
He whose vigour, at sea, was weakened by many afflictions
As he strove to win life for himself and return his comrades to their homes.
But not even he, for all this yearning, could save those comrades
For they were destroyed by their own immature foolishness
Having devoured the cattle of Helios, that son of Hyperion,
Who plucked from them the day of their returning.   (Odyssey, Book I, v. 1-9)

In addition, and importantly, Γαία, Earth Mother, is described in the Homeric hymn Εἰς Γῆν Μητέρα Πάντων as πρέσβιστος, the elder among beings, the mother of the gods, θεῶν μήτηρ, who nourishes all living beings:

γαῖαν παμμήτειραν ἀείσομαι ἠυθέμεθλον
πρεσβίστην ἣ φέρβει ἐπὶ χθονὶ πάνθ᾽ ὁπόσ᾽ ἐστίν

Even in the later mythoi associated with a monadic 'theos as creator' there is no divine law necessitating obedience and no humiliating fear of retribution by an omnipotent deity. Instead, as I noted in my *Classical Paganism And The Christian Ethos* in reference to tractate XI:3 of the Corpus Hermeticum,

"the sophia, the sapientia, of theos is presenced not in the 'word of God' (scriptures) but in the personal Greek virtues of τὸ ἀγαθὸν, τὸ καλὸν, and ἀρετὴ, and in the metaphysical principle denoted by the term αἰών."

Which leads to the understanding that in classical paganism mortals are considered to be connected to the cosmos, to the divine, to the numinous, through

> "not only reason (λόγος), perceiverance (νοῦς) and wordless-awareness (συμπάθεια, empathy) but also through τὸ ἀγαθὸν, τὸ καλὸν, and ἀρετὴ, through the beautiful and the well-balanced, the valourous and honourable, and those who possess arête, all of which are combined in one Greek phrase: καλὸς κἀγαθός, which means those who conduct themselves in a gentlemanly or lady-like manner." [14]

One such example is recounted by Xenophon:

> ἐκεῖνός γε μὴν ὑμνῶν οὔποτ' ἔληγεν ὡς τοὺς θεοὺς οἴοιτο οὐδὲν ἧττον ὁσίοις ἔργοις ἢ ἁγνοῖς ἱεροῖς ἥδεσθαι ἀλλὰ μὴν καὶ ὁπότε εὐτυχοίη οὐκ ἀνθρώπων ὑπερεφρόνει ἀλλὰ θεοῖς χάριν ᾔδει καὶ θαρρῶν πλείονα ἔθυεν ἢ ὀκνῶν ηὔχετο εἴθιστο δὲ φοβούμενος μὲν ἱλαρὸς φαίνεσθαι εὐτυχῶν δὲ πρᾷος εἶναι [Agesilaus, 11.2]

> this person, whom I praise, never ceased to believe that the gods delight in respectful deeds just as much as in consecrated temples, and, when blessed with success, he was never prideful but rather gave thanks to the gods. He also made more offerings to them when he was confident than supplications when he felt hesitant, and, in appearance, it was his habit to be cheerful when doubtful and mild-mannered when successful.

Those who conduct themselves in a refined, a gentlemanly or lady-like, manner are those who seek to avoid committing the error of hubris, ὕβρις, since they understand that hubris invites the attention of the Fates (Μοῖραι) and their ever heedful furies - Μοῖραι τρίμορφοι μνήμονές τ' Ἐρινύες - exemplifying as the female Fates and their Furies do an aspect of how mortals are connected to the cosmos, which cosmos is considered as living, as in Περὶ Εἱμαρμένης, attributed to Plutarch - τὸ φύσει διοικεῖσθαι τόνδε τὸν κόσμον σύμπνουν καὶ συμπαθῆ αὐτὸν αὑτῷ ὄντα (574e) - where the Kosmos is described as συμπαθῆ with itself and mutually breathing, σύμπνους.

In the classical mysticism described in tractate XIII of the Corpus Hermeticum [15], the pupil (τέκνον, son) is advised by his teacher (πάτερ, father) toward contemplation and thus toward a personal, an intimate, understanding of παλιγγενεσία, Palingenesis:

> ἐπίσπασαι εἰς ἑαυτόν, καὶ ἐλεύσεται· θέλησον, καὶ γίνεται· κατάργησον τοῦ σώματος τὰς αἰσθήσεις, καὶ ἔσται ἡ γένεσις τῆς θεότητος· κάθαραι σεαυτὸν ἀπὸ τῶν ἀλόγων τῆς ὕλης τιμωριῶν.

> Τιμωροὺς γὰρ ἐν ἐμαυτῷ ἔχω, ὦ πάτερ; Οὐκ ὀλίγους, ὦ τέκνον, ἀλλὰ καὶ φοβε ροὺς καὶ πολλούς. Ἀγνοῶ, ὦ πάτερ. Μία αὕτη, ὦ τέκνον, τιμωρία ἡ ἄγνοια· δευτέρα λύπη· τρίτη ἀκρασία· τετάρτη ἐπιθυμία· πέμπτη ἀδικία· ἕκτη πλεονεξία· ἑβδόμη ἀπάτη·

ὀγδόη φθόνος· ἐνάτη δόλος· δεκάτη ὀργή· ἐνδεκάτη προπέτεια·

δωδεκάτη κακία· εἰσὶ δὲ αὗται τὸν ἀριθμὸν δώδεκα· ὑπὸ δὲ ταύτας πλείονες ἄλλαι, ὦ τέκνον, διὰ τοῦ δεσμωτηρίου τοῦ σώματος αἰσθητικῶς πάσχειν ἀναγκάζουσι τὸν ἐνδιάθετον ἄνθρω πον· ἀφίστανται δὲ αὗται, οὐκ ἀθρόως, ἀπὸ τοῦ ἐλεηθέν τος ὑπὸ τοῦ θεοῦ, καὶ οὕτω συνίσταται ὁ τῆς παλιγγενε σίας τρόπος καὶ λόγος.

λοιπὸν σιώπησον, ὦ τέκνον, καὶ εὐφήμησον καὶ διὰ τοῦτο οὐ καταπαύσει τὸ ἔλεος εἰς ἡμᾶς ἀπὸ τοῦ θεοῦ· χαῖρε λοιπόν, ὦ τέκνον, ἀνακαθαιρό μενος ταῖς τοῦ θεοῦ δυνάμεσιν, εἰς συνάρθρωσιν τοῦ Λόγου. ἦλθεν ἡμῖν γνῶσις θεοῦ· ταύτης ἐλθούσης, ὦ τέκνον, ἐξηλάθη ἡ ἄγνοια. ἦλθεν ἡμῖν γνῶσις χαρᾶς· παραγενο μένης ταύτης, ὦ τέκνον, ἡ λύπη φεύξεται εἰς τοὺς χωροῦντας αὐτήν.

δύναμιν καλῶ ἐπὶ χαρᾷ τὴν ἐγ κράτειαν· ὦ δύναμις ἡδίστη, προσλάβωμεν, ὦ τέκνον, αὐτὴν ἀσμενέστατα· πῶς ἅμα τῷ παραγενέσθαι ἀπώσατο τὴν ἀκρασίαν; τετάρτην δὲ νῦν καλῶ καρτερίαν, τὴν κατὰ τῆς ἐπιθυμίας δύναμιν. ὁ βαθμὸς οὗτος, ὦ τέκνον, δικαιοσύνης ἐστὶν ἔδρασμα· χωρὶς γὰρ κρίσεως ἴδε πῶς τὴν ἀδικίαν ἐξήλασεν· ἐδικαιώθημεν, ὦ τέκνον, ἀδικίας ἀπού σης.

ἕκτην δύναμιν καλῶ εἰς ἡμᾶς, τὴν κατὰ τῆς πλεονεξίας, κοινωνίαν. ἀποστάσης δὲ ἔτι καλῶ τὴν ἀλήθειαν καὶ φεύγει ἀπάτη, ἀλήθεια παραγίνεται ἴδε πῶς τὸ ἀγαθὸν πεπλήρωται, ὦ τέκνον, παραγινομένης τῆς ἀληθείας· φθόνος γὰρ ἀφ᾿ ἡμῶν ἀπέστη· τῇ δὲ ἀληθείᾳ καὶ τὸ ἀγα θὸν ἐπεγένετο, ἅμα ζωῇ καὶ φωτί, καὶ οὐκέτι ἐπῆλθεν οὐδεμία τοῦ σκότους τιμωρία, ἀλλ᾿ ἐξέπτησαν νικηθεῖσαι ῥοίζῳ.

ἔγνωκας, ὦ τέκνον, τῆς παλιγγενεσίας τὸν τρόπον· τῆς δεκάδος παραγινομένης, ὦ τέκνον, συνετέθη νοερὰ γένεσις καὶ τὴν δωδεκάδα ἐξελαύνει καὶ ἐθεώθημεν τῇ γενέσει· ὅστις οὖν ἔτυχε κατὰ τὸ ἔλεος τῆς κατὰ θεὸν γενέσεως, τὴν σωματικὴν αἴσθησιν καταλιπών, ἑαυτὸν γνω ρίζει ἐκ τούτων συνιστάμενον καὶ εὐφραίνεται

Ἀκλινὴς γενόμενος ὑπὸ τοῦ θεοῦ, ὦ πάτερ, φαν τάζομαι, οὐχ ὁράσει ὀφθαλμῶν ἀλλὰ τῇ διὰ δυνάμεων νοη τικῇ ἐνεργείᾳ. ἐν οὐρανῷ εἰμι, ἐν γῇ, ἐν ὕδατι, ἐν ἀέρι· ἐν ζῴοις εἰμί, ἐν φυτοῖς· ἐν γαστρί, πρὸ γαστρός, μετὰ γασ τέρα, πανταχοῦ.

Tractate XIII, 7-11

Go within: and an arriving. Intend: and an engendering. Let physical perceptibility rest, and divinity will be brought-into-being. Refine yourself, away from the brutish Alastoras of Materies. [16]

Alastoras are within me, then, father?

Not just a few, my son, but many and terrifying.

I do not apprehend them, father.

My son, one Vengeress is Unknowing; the second, Grief. The third, Unrestraint; the fourth, Lascivity. The fifth, Unfairness; the sixth, Coveter. The seventh, Deceit; the eighth, Envy. The ninth, Treachery; the tenth, Wroth. The eleventh, Temerity; the twelfth, Putridity.

In number, these are twelve but below them are numerous others who, my son, compel the inner mortal - bodily incarcerated - to suffer because of perceptibility. But they absent themselves - although not all at once - from those to whom theos is generous, which is what the Way and Logos of Palingenesis consists of.

Henceforward, speak quietly, my son, and keep this secret. For thus may the generosity of theos toward us continue.

Henceforward, my son, be pleased, having refinement through the cræfts of theos to thus comprehend the Logos.

My son, to us: arrivance of Knowledge of Theos. On arrival: Unknowing is banished. My son, to us: arrivance of Knowledge of Delightfulness: on arriving, Grief runs away to those who have the room.

The influence invoked following Delightfulness is Self-Restraint: a most pleasant influence. Let us, my son, readily welcome her: arriving, she immediately pushes Unrestraint aside.

The fourth invoked is Perseverance who is influxious against Lascivity. Which Grade, my son, is the foundation of Ancestral Custom: observe how without any deliberation Unfairness was cast out. My son, we are vindicated since Unfairness has departed.

The sixth influence invoked for us - against Coveter - is community. With that departed, the next invokation: Actualis, and thus - with Actualis presenced - does Deceit run away. Observe, my son, how with Actualis presenced and Envy absent, the noble has been returned. For, following Actualis, there is the noble, together with Life and Phaos.

No more does the retribution of Skotos supervene, for, vanquished, they whirlingly rush away.

Thus, my son, you know the Way of Palingenesis. By the Dekad brought-into-being, geniture of apprehension was produced, banishing those twelve; and by this geniture we are of theos.

Thus whomsoever because of that generosity obtains divine geniture, having gone beyond physical perceptibility, discovers that they consist of such, and are pleased.

With a quietude, father, engendered by theos, the seeing is not of the sight from the eyes but that through the noetic actuosity of the cræft. I am in the Heavens; on Earth; in Water; in Air. I am in living beings, in plants; in the womb, before the womb, after the womb. Everywhere.

Which understanding of Palingenesis is of a personal, an interior, "moving away from the brutish Alastoras" involving a casting out of unfairness, a return to nobility, and an appreciation of Ancestral Custom [17]. Which 'moving away' is an interior anados.

A Human Numinosity

The paganus, Greco-Roman, apprehension of the numinous is thus profoundly human, individual in its immanency, subject to reason, to change, and to development. There is no eternally governing omnipotent deity since in classical mythoi even a governing god could be overthrown and replaced, as Zeus overthrew Kronos and as Kronos himself displaced his own father.

There is, in classical spirituality, no persecution of 'heretics' in the name of this or that interpretation of mythoi; no dogmatic scorn of women as there is in Tertullian and, for well over a thoiusand years, as there is in other Christian exegesists; no required meekness of submission to something or someone regarded as omnipotent; no concept of 'sin' as a punishable trangression of some immutable divine law, for even Zeus after his triumph only gave mortals a certain guidance:

> Ζῆνα δέ τις προφρόνως ἐπινίκια κλάζων
> τεύξεται φρενῶν τὸ πᾶν:
> ὃν φρονεῖν βροτοὺς ὁδώ-
> σαντα, τὸν πάθει μάθος
> θέντα κυρίως ἔχειν. Aeschylus: Agamemnon,174-183

> If anyone, from reasoning, exclaims loudly that victory of Zeus,
> Then they have acquired an understanding of all these things;
> Of he who guided mortals to reason,
> Who laid down that this possesses authority:
> Learning from adversity.

Which Zeus-given guidance - even though presencing his authority, and thus presencing the numinous in and for a certain Aeon - might be overturned, replaced, by a god or by a goddess who overthrew and replaced Zeus and who after their victory might well declaim a new Logos.

For the paganus, Greco-Roman, apprehension - and thus classical spirituality - was an apprehension, a spirituality, of evolution, of change, and of the necessity of harmonious balance, of avoidance of hubris. Of the virtue of ἀρετή understood as a μέσον (meson, median, a balance between 'being', actually existing, and 'not-being', a potentiality, as described by Aristotle (Metaphysics 9.1051a) and of perceiving, understanding, and seeking to be in balance with the harmonious 'cosmic order' (κόσμος) as appreciated by Cicero as a knowing (scientia) of what is divine and what is mortal:

> aequam igitur pronuntiabit sententiam ratio adhibita primum divinarum humanarumque rerum scientia, quae potest appellari rite sapientia, deinde adiunctis virtutibus, quas ratio rerum omnium dominas, tu voluptatum satellites et ministras esse voluisti. De Finibus Bonorum et Malorum, II, 37.

This balance is an aim of the anados, ἄνοδος - the mystical and individual journey of the mortal toward the numinous - described in the Poemandres tractate of the Corpus Hermeticum, during which journey the mortal sheds those traits of personality which are injurious to such an attainment:

> καὶ οὕτως ὁρμᾶι λοιπὸν ἄνω διὰ τῆς ἁρμονίας, καὶ τῆι πρώτηι ζώνηι δίδωσι τὴν αὐξητικὴν ἐνέργειαν καὶ τὴν μειωτικήν, καὶ τῆι δευτέραι τὴν μηχανὴν τῶν κακῶν, δόλον ἀνενέργητον, καὶ τῆι τρίτηι τὴν ἐπιθυμητικὴν ἀπάτην ἀνενέργητον, καὶ τῆι τετάρτηι τὴν ἀρχοντικὴν προφανίαν ἀπλεονέκτητον, καὶ τῆι πέμπτηι τὸ θράσος τὸ ἀνόσιον καὶ τῆς τόλμης τὴν προπέτειαν, καὶ τῆι ἕκτηι τὰς ἀφορμὰς τὰς κακὰς τοῦ πλούτου ἀνενεργήτους, καὶ τῆι ἑβδόμηι ζώνηι τὸ ἐνεδρεῦον ψεῦδος. Poemandres, 25

> Thus does the mortal hasten through the harmonious structure, offering up, in the first realm, that vigour which grows and which fades, and - in the second one - those dishonourable machinations, no longer functioning. In the third, that eagerness which deceives, no longer functioning; in the fourth, the arrogance of command, no longer insatiable; in the fifth, profane insolence and reckless haste; in the sixth, the bad inclinations occasioned by riches, no longer functioning; and in the seventh realm, the lies that lie in wait.

What is injurious to such a harmonious balance is what is dishonourable, with τὸ ἀγαθὸν - Summum Bonum - thus understood as honestum, as what is honourable, noble:

> summum bonum est quod honestum est; et quod magis admireris: unum bonum est, quod honestum est, cetera falsa et adulterina bona sunt. Seneca, Ad Lucilium Epistulae Morales, LXXI, 4.

> the greatest good is that which is honourable. Also - and you may wonder at this - only that which is honourable is good, with all other 'goods' simply false and deceitful.

An understanding also manifest in Cicero:

> Honestum igitur id intellegimus, quod tale est, ut detracta omni utilitate sine ullis praemiis fructibusve per se ipsum possit iure

laudari. quod quale sit, non tam definitione, qua sum usus, intellegi potest, quamquam aliquantum potest, quam communi omnium iudicio et optimi cuiusque studiis atque factis, qui permulta ob eam unam causam faciunt, quia decet, quia rectum, quia honestum est, etsi nullum consecuturum emolumentum vident. De Finibus Bonorum et Malorum, II, 45f.

For honestum is how hubris can be avoided and balance maintained, and is the essence of καλὸς κἀγαθός which presences the numinous, the divine, in and among mortals:

εἰ δύνασαι νοῆσαι τὸν θεόν, νοήσεις τὸ καλὸν καὶ ἀγαθόν […] ἐὰν περὶ τοῦ θεοῦ ζητῆις, καὶ περὶ τοῦ καλοῦ ζητεῖς μία γάρ ἐστιν εἰς αὐτὸ ἀποφέρουσα ὁδός, ἡ μετὰ γνώσεως εὐσέβεια.   Tractate VI, 5

If you are able to apprehend theos you can apprehend the beautiful and the noble [...] Thus a quest for theos is a quest for the beautiful, and there is only one path there: an awareness of the numinous combined with knowledge.

Furthermore, as stressed by Cicero in many of his writings, and as indicated by the quotation from tractate XIII of the Corpus Hermeticum - "the sixth influence invoked for us, against Coveter, is community" - an aspect of the paganus, Greco-Roman, apprehension of the numinous, of καλὸς κἀγαθός, is an awareness and acceptance of one's civic duties and responsibilities undertaken not because of any personal benefit (omni utilitate) that may result or be expected, and not because an omnioptent deity has, via some written texts, commanded it and will punish a refusal, but because it is the noble, the honourable - the gentlemanly, the lady-like, the human - thing to do.

o o o

III. Numinous Metaphysics

The ὑμνωδία κρύπτη λόγος Δ part of tractate XIII of the Corpus Hermeticum [18] provides a metaphysical insight into the paganus, Greco-Roman, apprehension of the numinous and thus into paganus spirituality.

Given in full in Appendix I, the song [19] begins with a polytheistic evocation: to Gaia, Earth, Trees, the Heavens, Air, and to Oceanus who brought "forth sweet water to where was inhabited and where was uninhabited to so sustain all mortals."

It addresses the Master Artisan, κτίσεως κύριον, the 'Founding Lord', who is τὸ πᾶν καὶ τὸ ἕν, 'all that exists' and 'The One', the monad, with τὸ πᾶν (literally, The All) a formulaic metaphysical phrase also occuring in tractate XII (τὸ πᾶν ἐν παντί) and in tractate XI which provides the metaphysical context:

> Ἄκουε, ὦ τέκνον, ὡς ἔχει ὁ θεὸς καὶ τὸ πᾶν. θεός, ὁ αἰών, ὁ κόσμος, ὁ χρόνος, ἡ γένεσις. ὁ θεὸς αἰῶνα ποιεῖ, ὁ αἰὼν δὲ τὸν κόσμον, ὁ κόσμος δὲ χρόνον, ὁ χρόνος δὲ γένεσιν. τοῦ δὲ θεοῦ ὥσπερ οὐσία ἐστὶ [τὸ ἀγαθόν, τὸ καλόν, ἡ εὐδαιμονία,] ἡ σοφία· τοῦ δὲ αἰῶνος ἡ ταυτότης· τοῦ δὲ κόσμου ἡ τάξις· τοῦ δὲ χρόνου ἡ μεταβολή· τῆς δὲ γενέσεως ἡ ζωὴ καὶ ὁ θάνατος

> Hear then, my son, of theos and of everything: theos, Aion, Kronos, Kosmos, geniture. Theos brought Aion into being; Aion: Kosmos; Kosmos, Kronos; Kronos, geniture. It is as if the quidditas of theos is actuality, honour, the beautiful, good fortune, Sophia. Of Aion, identity; of Kosmos, arrangement; of Kronos, variation; of geniture, Life and Death.

Which context is the harmonious, the ordered, structure of Reality, with ourselves as mortals connected to that-which is beyond us: in λόγος Δ to Gaia, Earth, Trees, the Heavens, and The One; and in tractate XI to Aion, Kronos, Kosmos, and importantly to geniture, to both Life and Death.

There is respect of (ancestral) custom; praise of virtues such as honesty; and a mortal gratitude:

> You, mastery, sing; and you, respectful of custom,
> Through me sing of such respect.
> Sing, my companions, for All That Exists:
> Honesty, through me, sing of being honest,
> The noble, sing of nobility.

Phaos and Life: fond celebration spreads from us to you.

My gratitude, father: actuosity of those my Arts.
My gratitude, theos: Artisan of my actuosities;
Through me, the Logos is sung for you.
Through me, may Kosmos accept
Such respectful wordful offerings as this.

Thus the apprehension, the spirituality, is uncomplicated, personal, devoid of dogma, restrained. As it is in the poem to Aphrodite by Sappho, quoted in Part II.

Numinous Criteria

If the numinous is a presencing, and an apprehension by us, of the divine, of the sacred, then is divinity, is the sacred, the sole domain of, a presencing of, the masculous - or such that the masculous dominates - or is it the domain of the muliebral; or the domain of such a balance between masculous and muliebral as the culture of pathei-mathos seems to indicate it is and should be. My own pathei-mathos certainly indicates that the numinous is primarily a manifestation of the muliebral and can be apprehended through a personal, an interior, balance between masculous and muliebral.

A masculous presencing is and has been manifest in a predominance of male deities; or in a dominant male deity; and/or in legends and myths which celebrate masculous values, such as competitiveness, a certain harshness, a desire to organize/control, a perceived conflict between some-thing, some abstraction, denoted 'good' and some-thing, some abstraction, denoted as 'evil', and a following of or an adherence to abstractions in general (such as a perceived divine law or some interpretation of religiosity) over and above personal love. Considered exoterically - not interiorly, not esoterically - a masculous presencing is manifest in a religion, with the attendant organized worship and devotion, with there existing a hierarchy, a creed or an article or articles of faith, and usually some texts, whether written or aural, regarded as sacred and/or as divinely inspired and which invariably require interpretation.

A muliebral presencing is or would be manifest in a predominance of female deities; or in a dominant female deity; in legends and myths which celebrate muliebral virtues, such as empathy, sensitivity, gentleness, compassion; and in the perception that personal love should triumph over and above adherence to abstractions. Considered exoterically - not interiorly, not esoterically - a muliebral presencing is manifest in a personal, varied, worship and devotion; in a personal weltanschauung and not in a religion; has no hierarchy; no creed, no article or articles of faith; and no texts whether written or aural.

Historically, it seems that revealed religions such as Christianity, Islam, and Judaism primarily manifest a presencing of the masculous where there is a male omnipotent deity whether named as God, Allah, or Jehovah; where the revelation and the interpretation of texts is taught primarily by men; where there is an eschatology of 'good' verses 'evil' with the consequent and perceived necessary conflicts and battles; with sentiments such as those by Tertullian in *De Cultu Feminarum* and in *De Monogamia* developed, and with such a presencing aptly described as patriarchal. In the case of Christianity, while some interpretations of it have in the past century slowly evolved to be somewhat more balanced in respect of the muliebral, it is still primarily a patriarchal presencing.

Historically, while the paganus apprehension of Greco-Roman culture was also primarily masculous it did presence aspects of the muliebral, manifest for example in female deities such as Athena, Artemis, and Gaia, and thus was somewhat more balanced, more harmonious in terms of re-presenting our human physis, than Christianity.

Thus a necessary question is how can (what I consider to be) a numinous balance between masculous and muliebral be metaphysically expressed, given that the culture of pathei-mathos has moved us, or can move us, beyond anthropomorphic deities, whether male or female; beyond myths and legends; beyond reliance on texts regarded as sacred and/or as divinely inspired; and even beyond the need for denotatum and religion.

Starting from the paganus apprehension described above, and using our human culture of pathei-mathos as a guide, such a metaphysics is (i) an (often wordless) awareness of ourselves as a fallible mortal, as a microcosmic connexion to other mortals, to other life, to Nature, and to the Cosmos beyond our world, and (ii) a new civitas, and one not based on some abstractive law but on a spiritual and interior (and thus not political) understanding and appreciation of our own Ancestral Culture and that of others; on our 'civic' duty to personally presence καλὸς κἀγαθός and thus to act and to live in a noble way. For the virtues of personal honour and manners, with their responsibilities, presence the fairness, the avoidance of hubris, the natural harmonious balance, the gender equality, the awareness and appreciation of the divine, that is the numinous.

---

[1] By religion is meant organized worship, devotion, and faith, where there is: (i) a belief in some deity/deities, or in some supreme Being or in some supra-personal power who/which can reward or punish the individual, and (ii) a distinction made between the realm of the sacred/the-gods/God/the-revered and the realm of the ordinary or the human.

The term organized here implies an established institution, body or group - or a plurality of these - who or which has at least to some degree codified the faith and/or the acts of worship and devotion, and which is accepted as having some authority or has established some authority among the adherents. This codification is founded on accepting as authoritative certain writings (texts) and/or a certain book or books.

[2] *De Pudicitia*, X, 12.

[3] The archaeological - the physical - evidence seems to indicate that the Greek text of the Old Testament is older than the Hebrew text, with the earliest manuscript fragment being Greek Papyrus 458 currently housed in the Rylands Papyri collection - qv. Bulletin of the John Rylands Library, 20 (1936), pp. 219-45 - and which fragment was discovered in Egypt and has been dated as being from the second century BCE.

In contrast, the earliest fragments of the Old Testament in Hebrew date from c.150 BCE to c. 70 CE, and are part of what has come to be known as the Dead Sea Scrolls. In addition, the earliest known Greek - and almost complete - text of the Old Testament, Codex Vaticanus, dates from c.320 CE with the earliest complete Hebrew text of the Tanakh, the Allepo Codex, dating from centuries later, around 920 CE.

While it is and has been a common presumption that the Hebrew version of the Old Testament is older than the Greek version, my inclination is to favour the extant physical evidence over and above presumption. Were physical evidence of Hebrew texts earlier than Greek Papyrus 458 discovered, and of there existing a complete Hebrew text dating from before Codex Vaticanus, my inclination would be to revise my opinion based on a study of the new evidence.

[4] *De Monogamia*, VII, 1.

[5] Tertullian, *De Cultu Feminarum*, I, 2.

[6] The Latin word translated by nexion is *ianua*, which implies a gateway, a door, an entrance. The Latin translated "You are The Resignatrix of The Tree" is *tu es arboris illius resignatrix*, with resignatrix here - as with the preceding *ianua* - suggestive of a title, of the woman who broke the seal affixed to the forbidden fruit of the Tree Of Knowledge. A more literal translation of the

following *tu es diuinae legis prima desertrix* is: You are the first to forsake Divine Decree.

The three phrases *tu es diaboli ianua, tu es arboris illius resignatrix, tu es diuinae legis prima desertrix*, read as if they might be some 'evil' heathen incantation, which might have been Tertullian's intent.

[7] As described in my 'philosophy of pathei-mathos', I use the term physis, φύσις, contextually to refer to:

> (i) the ontology of beings, an ontology - a reality, a 'true nature '- that is often obscured by denotatum and by abstractions, both of which conceal physis;
> (ii) the relationship between beings, and between beings and Being, which is of us - we mortals - as a nexion, an affective effluvium (or emanation) of Life (ψυχή) and thus of why 'the separation-of-otherness' is a concealment of that relationship;
> (iii) the character, or persona, of human beings, and which character - sans denotatum - can be discovered (revealed, known) by the faculty of empathy;
> (iv) the unity - the being - beyond the division of our physis, as individual mortals, into masculous and muliebral;
> (v) that manifestation denoted by the concept Time, with Time considered to be an expression/manifestation of the physis of beings.

I use the term denotatum - from the Latin, denotare - in accord with its general meaning which is "to denote or to describe by an expression or a word; to name some-thing; to refer that which is so named or so denoted."

Thus understood, and used as an Anglicized term, denotatum is applicable to both singular and plural instances and thus obviates the need to employ the Latin plural denotata.

In respect of the term numinous, it derives from the classical Latin numen which denoted "a reverence for the divine; a divinity; divine power". Numen has been used in English since the 15th century, with 'numinous' dating from the middle of the 17th century and used to signify "of or relating to a numen; revealing or indicating the presence of a divinity; divine, spiritual."

As noted in my *The Numinous Way Of Pathei-Mathos,* I use it to additonally describe

> "what manifests or can manifest or remind us of (what can reveal) the natural balance of ψυχή; a balance which ὕβρις upsets. This natural balance – our being as human beings – is or can be manifest to us in or by what is harmonious, or what reminds us of what is harmonious and beautiful. In a practical way, it is what we regard or come to appreciate as 'sacred' and dignified; what expresses our developed

humanity and thus places us, as individuals, in our correct relation to ψυχή, and which relation is that we are but one mortal emanation of ψυχή."

[8] Volume I (chapters 1-4) of my translation of and commentary on the Gospel According To John was published in July 2017 with volume II (chapters 5-10) scheduled for publication in 2019.

A version in html – including chapter 5, which is subject to revision and updated as and when new verses and the associated commentary are available – is (as of October 2017) at http://www.davidmyatt.info/gospel-john.html

[9] What follows is a (slightly edited) extract from my commentary on John 3:16-21.

° *Nomos.* νόμος. A transliteration since as with 'logos' a particular metaphysical principle is implied and one which requires contextual interpretation; a sense somewhat lost if the English word 'law' is used especially given what the word 'law' often now imputes.

° *Phaos.* Given that φάος metaphorically (qv. Iliad, Odyssey, Hesiod, etcetera) implies the being, the life, 'the spark', of mortals, and, generally, either (i) the illumination, the light, that arises because of the Sun and distinguishes the day from the night, or (ii) any brightness that provides illumination and thus enables things to be seen, I am inclined to avoid the vague English word 'light' which all other translations use and which, as in the case of God, has, in the context of the evangel of Jesus of Nazareth, acquired particular meanings mostly as a result of centuries of exegesis and which therefore conveys or might convey something that the Greek word, as used by the author of this particular Greek text, might not have done.

Hence my transliteration – using the Homeric φάος instead of φῶς – and which transliteration requires the reader to pause and consider what phaos may, or may not, mean, suggest, or imply. As in the matter of logos, it is most probably not some sort of philosophical principle, neo-Platonist or otherwise.

Interestingly, φῶς occurs in conjunction with ζωή and θεὸς and ἐγένετο and Ἄνθρωπος in the *Corpus Hermeticum*, thus echoing the evangel of John:

> φῶς καὶ ζωή ἐστιν ὁ θεὸς καὶ πατήρ, ἐξ οὗ ἐγένετο ὁ Ἄνθρωπος (Poemandres, 1.21)

> Life and phaos are [both] of Theos, The Father, Who brought human beings into existence

° *For their deeds were harmful.* ἦν γὰρ αὐτῶν πονηρὰ τὰ ἔργα. Harmful: that is, caused pain and suffering. To impute to πονηρός here the meaning of a moral abstract 'evil' is, in my view, mistaken. Similarly with the following φαῦλος in v.20 which imparts the sense of being 'mean', indifferent.

Since the Phaos is Jesus, those who are mean, those who do harm, avoid Jesus because (qv. 2.25) he – as the only begotten son of Theos – knows the person within and all their deeds. Thus, fearing being exposed, they avoid him, and thus cannot put their trust in him and so are condemned and therefore lose the opportunity of eternal life.

° *whomsoever practices disclosure.* ὁ δὲ ποιῶν τὴν ἀλήθειαν. Literally, 'they practising the disclosing.' That is, those who disclose – who do not hide – who they are and what deeds they have done, and who thus have no reason to fear exposure. Here, as in vv.19-20, the meaning is personal – about the character of people – and not about abstractions such as "evil" and "truth", just as in previous verses it is about trusting in the character of Jesus. Hence why here ἀλήθεια is 'sincerity', a disclosing, a revealing – the opposite of lying and of being deceitful – and not some impersonal 'truth'.

[10] Note how Jesus does not disapprovingly preach about – does not even mention – the apparently superstitious practice of infirm individuals waiting by a 'miraculous' pool in order to be cured.

[11] A (slightly edited) extract from my commentary on John 5:1-16.

° *the place of the sheep.* Since the Greek προβατικός means "of or relating to sheep" and there is no mention of a 'gate' (or of anything specific such as a market) I prefer a more literal translation. It is a reasonable assumption that the sheep were, and had in previous times been, kept there prior to being offered as sacrifices, as for example sheep are still so held in particular places in Mecca during Eid al-Adha, the Muslim feast of sacrifice.

° *named in the language of the Hebrews.* ἐπιλεγομένη Ἑβραϊστὶ.

° *the infirm.* The Greek word ἀσθενέω implies those lacking normal physical strength.

° *awaiting a change in the water.* Reading ἐκδεχομένων τὴν τοῦ ὕδατος κίνησιν with the Textus Receptus, omitted by NA28, but included in the Anglo-Saxon version, by Tyndale and Wycliffe.

° *Envoy of Theos.* Reading ἄγγελος γάρ κυρίου κατά καιρῶν κατέβαινεν (qv. Cyril of Alexandria, Commentary on John, Book II, V, 1-4, Migne Patrologia Graeca 73) and ἐν τῇ κολυμβήθρᾳ, καὶ ἐτάρασσεν τὸ ὕδωρ· ὁ οὖν πρῶτος ἐμβὰς μετὰ τὴν ταραχὴν τοῦ ὕδατος, ὑγιὴς ἐγίνετο, ᾧ δήποτε κατειχετο νοσήματι with the Textus Receptus. The verse is omitted by NA28, but included in ASV, Tyndale, and Wycliffe.

   a) *envoy.* As noted in the commentary on 1:51, interpreting ἄγγελος as 'envoy' (of theos) and not as 'angel', particularly given the much later Christian iconography associated with the term 'angel'.

b) *Theos*. Regarding ἄγγελος γὰρ κυρίου, qv. Matthew 28.2 ἄγγελος γὰρ κυρίου καταβὰς ἐξ οὐρανοῦ, "an envoy of [the] Lord/Master descended from Empyrean/the heavens." Since here κύριος implies Theos (cf. John 20.28 where it is used in reference to Jesus), an interpretation such as "envoy of Theos" avoids both the phrase "envoy of the Master" – which is unsuitable given the modern connotations of the word 'master' – and the exegetical phrase "angel/envoy of the Lord" with all its associated and much later iconography both literal, by means of Art, and figurative, in terms of one's imagination. An alternative expression would be "envoy of the Domine," with Domine (from the Latin Dominus) used in English as both a respectful form of address and as signifying the authority of the person or a deity.

c) *became complete*. ὑγιὴς ἐγίνετο. The suggestion is of the person becoming 'whole', complete, *sanus*, and thus ceasing to be 'broken', incomplete, infirm.

° *bedroll*. κράβαττος (Latin, grabatus) has no suitable equivalent in English since in context it refers to the portable bed and bedding of the infirm. The nearest English approximation is bedroll.

° *And, directly, the man became complete*. καὶ εὐθέως ἐγένετο ὑγιὴς ὁ ἄνθρωπος. Metaphysically, the Evangelist is implying that 'completeness' – wholeness – for both the healthy and the infirm (whether infirm because of sickness or a physical infirmity) arises because of and through Jesus.

° *treated*. Taking the literal sense of θεραπεύω here. Hence: cared for, treated, attended to. As a healer or a physician might care for, treat, or attend to, someone.

° *no more missteps*. μηκέτι ἁμάρτανε. That is, make no more mistakes in judgement or in deeds. Qv. the Introduction [to Volume I of the translation] regarding translating ἁμαρτία in a theologically neutral way as 'mistake' or 'error' instead of by the now exegetical English word 'sin'. Cf. 1.29, 8.7, et seq.

° *Judaeans*. Qv. my essay *A Note On The Term Jews In The Gospel of John*, which is included here as an appendix

° *harass*. διώκω. Cf. the Latin *persequor*, for the implication is of continually 'following' and pursuing him in order to not only try and worry or distress him but also (as becomes evident) to find what they regard is evidence against him in order to have him killed, qv. 5.18, 7.1, 7.19 et seq.

[12] Ἱερός Λόγος: *An Esoteric Mythos*. Included in: David Myatt, *Corpus Hermeticum: Eight Tractates: Translation and Commentary*, 2017.

[13] The culture of pathei-mathos is described in Appendix III.

[14] Myatt, David. *Classical Paganism And The Christian Ethos*. 2017. p.27.

[15] This hermetic tractate, as so many others, employs a technical - an esoteric - vocabulary. Thus terms such as νοερός, ἀσφίγγωτος, ἐνέργεια, ἐνδιάθετον ἄνθρω - to name but a few - require contextual interpretation and avoidance of such common English words (for example, 'intellectual', and energy) as may impose modern meanings on such an ancient text.

The commentary which accompanies my translation of tractate XIII - in *Corpus Hermeticum: Eight Tractates* - provides the relevant context and an explanation of my translating choices such as Actualis and cræft.

[16] As noted in the commentary on my translation I have chosen to personify τιμωρία, partly in reference to Clytemnestra as depicted by Aeschylus:

> *alastoras.* Since the Greek word τιμωρία is specific and personal, implying vengeance, retribution, and also a divine punishment, it seems apposite to try and keep, in English, the personal sense even though no specific deeds or deeds are mentioned in the text, but especially because of what follows: Τιμωροὺς γὰρ ἐν ἐμαυτῷ ἔχω, ὦ πάτερ. Hence my interpretation, "the brutish alastoras of Materies," using the English term alastoras - singular, *alastor*, from the Greek ἀλάστωρ, an avenging deity, and also a person who avenges certain deeds. Qv. Aeschylus, Agamemnon, 1497-1508.

> *materies.* ὕλη. A variant form of the Latin *materia*, thus avoiding the English word 'matter' which now has connotations, derived from sciences such as Physics, that are not or may not be relevant here. In addition, the term requires contextual, metaphysical, interpretation, for as used here it may or may not be equivalent to the ὕλη of Poemandres 10, of III:1, και τα λοιπά. Hence why I have here chosen 'materies' rather than - as in those other tractates - 'substance'.

[17] The goddess Δίκη - qv. Hesiod, Ἔργα καὶ Ἡμέραι, vv 213-218 - is the goddess of Fairness and of Tradition manifest as Tradition is in Ancestral Custom(s). The usual translation of δίκη is Justice or Judgement which English terms, with their various post Greco-Roman and modern abstractive and legal connotations, are in my view rather misleading.

[18] I incline toward the view that the song, begun in section 17, ends in section 18, an ending signalled by the expression at the beginning of section 19, "such is what the Arts within me loudly call out," ταῦτα βοῶσιν αἱ δυνάμεις αἱ ἐν ἐμοί. Sections 19-21 thus being a personal exegesis.

[19] Crucial in understanding the paganus nature of the song are the term

ὕμνος and the lines οὗτός ἐστιν ὁ τοῦ νοῦ ὀφθαλμός, καὶ δέξαιτο τῶν δυνάμεων μου τὴν εὐλογίαν. αἱ δυνάμεις αἱ ἐν ἐμοί, ὑμνεῖτε τὸ ἓν καὶ τὸ πᾶνί.

Given that the English term 'hymn' is now commonly associated with Christianity it is in my view an unsataisfactory translation of ὕμνος in this as in other tractates of the Corpus Hermeticum especially as ὕμνος was used by Homer in The Odyssey (VIII, 428-9) in association with enjoying a splendid feast, τά οἱ Φαίηκες ἀμύμονες ἐνθάδ᾽ ἔνεικαν δαιτί τε τέρπηται καὶ ἀοιδῆς ὕμνον ἀκούων, where 'song' is an appropriate translation, as it is in this tractate.

To appreciate the aforementioned lines in the apposite cultural and textual context, is to understand that δυνάμεων is not, in this tractate and in some others, suggestive of 'power' possessed by an individual - as in the egoistic 'my powers' - but rather a skill, an ability, craft, an art, that has been cultivated and learnt as in a person learning the art of chanson.

Hence my reading of those lines as:

> May the one who is the eye of perceiveration accept this fond celebration
> From my Arts.
> Let those Arts within me sing for The One and for All That Exists.

Which is in contrast to the conventional interpretation, which is along the following lines: "He is the mind's eye. May he accept praise from my powers. Powers with me sing a hymn to the one and to the universe."

Appendix I

Logos Δ. The Esoteric Song

Cantio Arcana

υμνωδία κρύπτη λόγος Δ

πᾶσα φύσις κόσμου προσδεχέσθω τοῦ ὕμνου τὴν ἀκοήν. ἀνοίγηθι γῆ, ἀνοιγήτω μοι πᾶς μοχλὸς ὄμβρου, τὰ δένδρα μὴ σείεσθε. ὑμνεῖν μέλλω τὸν τῆς κτίσεως κύριον, καὶ τὸ πᾶν καὶ τὸ ἕν. ἀνοίγητε οὐρανοί, ἄνεμοί τε στῆτε. ὁ κύκλος ὁ ἀθάνατος τοῦ θεοῦ, προσδεξάσθω μου τὸν λόγον· μέλλω γὰρ ὑμνεῖν τὸν κτίσαντα τὰ πάντα, τὸν πήξαντα τὴν γῆν καὶ οὐρανὸν κρεμάσαντα καὶ ἐπιτάξαντα ἐκ τοῦ ὠκεα νοῦ τὸ γλυκὺ ὕδωρ εἰς τὴν οἰκουμένην καὶ ἀοίκητον ὑπάρ χειν εἰς διατροφὴν καὶ κτίσιν πάντων τῶν ἀνθρώπων, τὸν ἐπιτάξαντα πῦρ

φανῆναι εἰς πᾶσαν πρᾶξιν θεοῖς τε καὶ ἀνθρώποις.   δῶμεν πάντες ὁμοῦ αὐτῷ
τὴν εὐλογίαν, τῷ ἐπὶ τῶν οὐρανῶν μετεώρῳ, τῷ πάσης φύσεως κτίστῃ.

οὗτός ἐστιν ὁ τοῦ νοῦ ὀφθαλμός, καὶ δέξαιτο τῶν δυνάμεων μου τὴν εὐλογίαν.
αἱ δυνάμεις αἱ ἐν ἐμοί, ὑμνεῖτε τὸ ἓν καὶ τὸ πᾶν· συνάσατε τῷ θελήματί μου
πᾶσαι αἱ ἐν ἐμοὶ δυνάμεις. γνῶσις ἁγία, φωτισθεὶς ἀπὸ σοῦ, διὰ σοῦ τὸ νοητὸν
φῶς ὑμνῶν χαίρω ἐν χαρᾷ νοῦ. πᾶσαι δυνάμεις ὑμνεῖτε σὺν ἐμοί. καὶ σύ μοι,
ἐγκράτεια, ὕμνει. δικαιοσύνη μου, τὸ δίκαιον ὕμνει δι᾿ ἐμοῦ. κοινωνία ἡ ἐμή, τὸ
πᾶν ὕμνει δι᾿ ἐμοῦ· ὕμνει ἀλήθεια τὴν ἀλήθειαν. τὸ ἀγαθόν, ἀγαθόν, ὕμνει· ζωὴ
καὶ φῶς, ἀφ᾿ ὑμῶν εἰς ὑμᾶς χωρεῖ ἡ εὐλογία. εὐχαριστῶ σοι, πάτερ, ἐνέργεια
τῶν δυνάμεων. εὐχαριστῶ σοι, θεέ, δύναμις τῶν ἐνεργειῶν μου· ὁ σὸς Λόγος δι᾿
ἐμοῦ ὑμνεῖ σέ. δι᾿ ἐμοῦ δέξαι τὸ πᾶν λόγῳ, λογικὴν θυσίαν.

Let every Physis of Kosmos favourably listen to this song.
Gaia: be open, so that every defence against the Abyss is opened for me;
Trees: do not incurvate;
For I now will sing for the Master Artisan,
For All That Exists, and for The One.

Open: you Celestial Ones; and you, The Winds, be calm.
Let the deathless clan of theos accept this, my logos.
For I shall sing of the maker of everything;
Of who established the Earth,
Of who affixed the Heavens,
Of who decreed that Oceanus should bring forth sweet water
To where was inhabited and where was uninhabited
To so sustain all mortals;
Of who decreed that Fire should bring light
To divinities and mortals for their every use.

Let us all join in fond celebration of who is far beyond the Heavens:
That artisan of every Physis.

May the one who is the eye of perceiveration accept this fond celebration
From my Arts.

Let those Arts within me sing for The One and for All That Exists
As I desire all those Arts within me to blend, together.

Numinous knowledge, from you a numinal understanding:
Through you, a song of apprehended phaos,
Delighted with delightful perceiverance.
Join me, all you Arts, in song.

You, mastery, sing; and you, respectful of custom,
Through me sing of such respect.

Sing, my companions, for All That Exists:
Honesty, through me, sing of being honest,
The noble, sing of nobility.

Phaos and Life: fond celebration spreads from us to you.

My gratitude, father: actuosity of those my Arts.
My gratitude, theos: Artisan of my actuosities;
Through me, the Logos is sung for you.
Through me, may Kosmos accept
Such respectful wordful offerings as this.

Appendix II

A Note On The Term Jews In The Gospel of John

In the past century or so there has been much discussion about the term 'the Jews' in standard English translations of the Gospel of John and thus whether or not the Gospel portrays Jews in a negative way given such words about them as the following, from the translation known as the Douay-Rheims Bible:

> You are of your father the devil, and the desires of your father you will do. He was a murderer from the beginning, and he stood not in the truth; because truth is not in him. When he speaketh a lie, he speaketh of his own: for he is a liar, and the father thereof. (8.44)

In the Gospel of John the term οἱ Ἰουδαῖοι first occurs in verse 19 of chapter one:

> ὅτε ἀπέστειλαν πρὸς αὐτὸν οἱ Ἰουδαῖοι ἐξ Ἱεροσολύμων ἱερεῖς καὶ Λευίτας ἵνα ἐρωτήσωσιν αὐτόν

In the Douay-Rheims Bible this is translated as: "when the Jews sent from Jerusalem priests and Levites to him." In the King James Bible: "when the Jews sent priests and Levites from Jerusalem to ask him."

In my translation of John – a work in progress [1] – I translated as: "when the Judaeans dispatched priests and Levites from Jerusalem to ask him."

For, after much consideration, I chose – perhaps controversially – to translate ἰουδαία by Judaeans, given (i) that the English terms Jews and Jewish (deriving from the 13th/14th century words gyv/gyw and Iewe) have acquired connotations (modern and medieval) which are not relevant to the period under consideration; and (ii) that the Greek term derives from a place name, Judaea (as does the Latin iudaeus); and (iii) that the Anglo-Saxon version (ASV) retains the sense of the Greek: here (iudeas) as elsewhere, as for example at 2.6, æfter iudea geclensunge, "according to Judaean cleansing."

Such a translation not only dispenses with the "portraying Jews in a negative way" discussion but also reveals a consistent narrative, with the Evangelist not writing that "the Jews" saught to kill Jesus, but only that some Judaeans desired to do so. In addition, as the story of the Samarian (Samaritan) woman in chapter 4 makes clear, it places into perspective the difference between Judaea, Samaria, and Galilee, and why the Evangelist narrates that it was "necessary" for Jesus to pass through Samaria on the way to Galilee, Ἔδει δὲ αὐτὸν διέρχεσθαι διὰ τῆς Σαμαρείας.

Given what follows (chapter 4 vv.9-10) this suggests a certain historical antipathy between the people of Judaea and the people of Samaria even though the Samarians – as is apparent from the Gospel – shared many, but not all, of the religious traditions of the Judaeans, as did most of the people of Galilee, including Jesus. Since the Evangelist specifically writes that it was Judaeans who saught to kill Jesus (5.18; 7.1; 7.19 et seq) it seems as if the antipathy by Judaeans to Jesus of Nazareth in particular and to Samarians in general – with the Evangelist stating that Judaeans would not share or make use of (συγχράομαι) Samarian things – arose from Judaeans in general believing that their religious practices based on their particular interpretation of the religion of Moses and the Prophets were correct and that they themselves as a result were 'righteous' – better than Samarians – with Jesus the Galilean considered by many Judaeans, and certainly by the priestly authorities, as having committed (qv. 10.33) 'blasphemy' (βλασφημία) and thus should be killed.

Such differing religious traditions, such internecine feuds, such religious fanaticism and intolerance on behalf of some Judaeans – an intolerance exemplified also when (qv. 10.22) one of the guards of Caiaphas the High Priest (Καιάφαν τὸν ἀρχιερέα) physically assaults Jesus for not showing the High Priest "due deference" – exemplifies why in this Gospel ιουδαία should be translated not by the conventional term 'Jews' but rather by Judaeans.

∘∘∘

In respect of the term ιουδαία, it is interesting to consider two writings by Flavius Josephus, and one by Cassius Dio Cocceianus (dating from c.230 CE). The two works by Josephus are conventionally entitled 'Antiquities of the Jews' (c. 93 CE) and 'The Jewish Wars' (c. 75 CE) although I incline toward the view that such titles are incorrect and that the former – entitled in Greek, Ιουδαικης αρχαιολογιας – should be 'Judaean Antiquities', while the latter – entitled in Greek, Ἱστορία Ἰουδαϊκοῦ πολέμου πρὸς Ῥωμαίου – should be 'History of the Conflict Between Judaeans and Romaeans', and this because of how Josephus, in those works, describes himself and that conflict.

Ιουδαικης αρχαιολογιας

In this work Josephus wrote:

1.4 τούτων δὴ τῶν προειρημένων αἰτιῶν αἱ τελευταῖαι δύο κἀμοὶ συμβεβήκασι· τὸν μὲν γὰρ πρὸς τοὺς Ῥωμαίους πόλεμον ἡμῖν τοῖς Ἰουδαίοις γενόμενον [...]

1.5 διάταξιν τοῦ πολιτεύματος ἐκ τῶν Ἑβραϊκῶν μεθηρμηνευμένην γραμμάτων [...]

1.6 δηλῶσαι τίνες ὄντες ἐξ ἀρχῆς Ἰουδαῖοι

a) 1.4. τὸν μὲν γὰρ πρὸς τοὺς Ῥωμαίους πόλεμον ἡμῖν τοῖς Ἰουδαίοις γενόμενον, "how that conflict between Romaeans and we Judaeans came about."

To be pedantic, Ῥωμαίους – Romaeans – implies those "of Rome". That is, the word suggests those associated with a particular place, as does the term Judaeans. Which association of people with a particular place or region is historically germane.

b) 1.5. διάταξιν τοῦ πολιτεύματος τῶν Ἑβραϊκῶν μεθηρμηνευμένην γραμμάτων, "the decrees of our civitatium as expounded in the writings of the Hebrews." Less literally, "the laws of our communities as expounded in the writings of the Hebrews."

Thus he does not write about the "Jewish scriptures" or about "the scriptures of the Jews", even though the consensus is that γραφῇ here – as throughout the New Testament – has the meaning 'scripture' rather than its normal sense of 'that which is written', with the English word 'scripture' (usually written with a capital S) having the specific meaning "the writings of the Old and/or of the New Testament". However, this specific meaning only dates back to c.1300 and was used by Wycliffe in his 1389 translation, from whence, via Tyndale, it was used in the King James version. Prior to 1300, the ASV has *gewrite* – 'what was written', writing, inscription – with the Latin of Jerome having *scripturae*, as does Codex Palatinus of the earlier Vetus Latina. [2] Classically understood, the Latin has the same meaning as the Greek γραφῇ: writing, something written, an inscription. [3]

c) 1.6 δηλῶσαι τίνες ὄντες ἐξ ἀρχῆς Ἰουδαῖοι, "to make known how Judaeans came about."

Ἱστορία Ἰουδαϊκοῦ πολέμου πρὸς Ῥωμαίου

In the Προοίμιον of this book Josephus wrote:

a) Ἰώσηπος Ματθίου παῖς ἐξ Ἱεροσολύμων ἱερεύς

That is, Josephus describes himself as "the son of Matthias, a priest, from Jerusalem." He does not write that he is "Jewish" and nor does he write that he is from Judaea.

b) σχεδὸν δὲ καὶ ὧν ἀκοῇ παρειλήφαμεν ἢ πόλεων πρὸς πόλεις ἢ ἐθνῶν ἔθνεσι συρραγέντων.

A conventional translation would have πόλις as 'city' and ἔθνος as 'nation' so that the latter part would conventionally be translated along the following lines: "cities would have fought against cities, or nations against nations."

However, the terms 'nation' and 'city' are or can be misleading, given their modern connotations, whereas a historical approximation for ἔθνος would be 'tribe', 'people', or 'community', and for πόλις – understood here as referring to a particular named place with a history of settlement – town, fortified town, burg, borough, municipality. Such choices would produce a translation such as: "municipality would have fought municipality, community with community." The evocation is thus more parochial, more regional, as befits the historical past and the context: here, an insurrection, a conflict between the people of Judaea and the armed forces commanded by Roman citizens (those "of Rome") duly appointed to positions of power.

Regarding The Term Ἰουδαικός

While the term is conventionally cited as meaning Jewish – although LSJ provides no sources, with the English words 'Jew' and 'Jewish' not existing until the 13th/14th century CE – the sense of the term in Ῥωμαϊκὴ Ἱστορία by Cassius Dio Cocceianus (for example, 67.14.2, 68.1.2) is Judaean, referring to the people of Judaea and their customs and way of life, Ἰουδαϊκοῦ βίου, τῶν Ἰουδαίων ἤθη:

> ὑφ᾿ ἧς καὶ ἄλλοι ἐς τὰ τῶν Ἰουδαίων ἤθη ἐξοκέλλοντες πολλοὶ κατεδικάσθησαν καὶ οἱ μὲν ἀπέθανον οἱ δὲ τῶν γοῦν οὐσιῶν ἐστερήθησαν (67.14.2)

ooo

Conclusion

As noted in the Preface to my translation of The Gospel of John, I have endeavoured to avoid reading into the text the meanings that some of the English words conventionally used in other translations – and given in lexicons – may now suggest, or do suggest often as a result of over a thousand years of exegesis. In the matter of ιουδαία the translation by the relatively recent term 'Jews' has suggested meanings which, at least in my fallible opinion, are irrelevant to the milieu of the Gospels and which thus distorts, or which can distort, the narrative of the Gospel of John.

[1] As of July 2017, the translation of and a commentary on chapters one to four of The Gospel of John have been completed, which partial translation and commentary is available at: https://davidmyatt.wordpress.com/gospel-according-to-john/

[2] For context, the verse in the Latin version of Jerome is: cum ergo resurrexisset a mortuis recordati sunt discipuli eius quia hoc dicebat et crediderunt scripturae et sermoni quem dixit iesus.

The Latin of Codex Palatinus, Vetus Latina: Cum ergo resurrexit a mortuis commonefacti sunt discipuli eius quoniam hoc dicebat et crediderunt scripturae et sermoni quem dixit IHS.

The Latin of Codex Brixianusis, Vetus Latina: cum ergo resurre xisset a mortuis recordati sunt discipuli eius quia hoc dixerat et crediderunt scribturae et sermoni quem dixit IHS.

[3] Qv. Tacitus: "non diurna actorum scriptura reperio ullo insigni officio functam." *Annals*, Book III, 3.

Appendix III

Suffering And The Human Culture Of Pathei-Mathos

This is an extract from a written reply, in September 2013, to a personal correspondent. It has been revised for inclusion here, with some footnotes added in an effort to elucidate some parts of the text.

In respect of the question whether I am optimistic about our future as a species, I vacillate between optimism and pessimism, knowing as I - and so many - do from experience that the world contains people who do good things [1], people who do bad things, and people who when influenced or led or swayed by some-thing or someone can veer either way; and given that it seems as if in each generation there are those - many - who have not learned or who cannot learn from the pathei-mathos of previous generations, from our collective human πάθει μάθος that has brought-into-being a culture of pathei-mathos thousands of years old. Historically - prior to, during after the time of Cicero, and over a thousand years later during and after the European Renaissance - this culture was evident in Studia Humanitatis, and is now presenced in works inspired by or recollecting personal pathei-mathos and described in memoirs, aural stories, and historical accounts; in particular works of literature, poetry, and drama; in non-verbal mediums such as music and Art, and by art-forms such as films and documentaries.

This culture of pathei-mathos reveals to us the beauty, the numinosity, of personal love; the numinosity of humility, and compassion; and the tragic lamentable unnecessary suffering caused by hubris, dishonour, selfishness, inconsiderance, intolerance, prejudice, hatred, war, extremism, and ideologies [2]. A world-wide suffering so evident, today, for example in the treatment of and the violence (by men) toward women; in the continuing armed conflicts - regional and local, over some-thing - that displace tens of thousands of people and cause destruction, injury, and hundreds of thousands of deaths; and evident also in the killing of innocent people [3] by those who adhere to a harsh interpretation of some religion or some political ideology.

Do good people, world-wide, outweigh bad ones? My experiences and travels incline me to believe they may do, although it seems as if the damage the bad ones do, the suffering they cause, sometimes and for a while outweighs the good that others do. But does the good done, in societies world-wide, now outweigh the bad done, especially such large-scale suffering as is caused by despots, corruption, armed conflict, and repressive regimes? Probably, at least in some societies. And yet even in such societies where, for example, education is widespread, there always seem to be selfish, dishonourable, inconsiderate, people; and also people such as the extremist I was with my hubriatic certitude-of-knowing inciting or causing hatred and violence and intolerance and glorifying war and kampf and trying to justify killing in the name of some abstraction or some belief or some cause or some ideology. People mostly, it seems, immune to and/or intolerant of the learning of the culture of pathei-mathos; a learning available to us in literature, music, Art, memoirs, in the aural and written recollections of those who endured or who witnessed hatred, violence, intolerance, conflict, war, and killing, and a learning also available in the spiritual message of those who taught humility, goodness, love, and tolerance. Immune or intolerant people who apparently can only change - or who could only possibly change for the better - only when they themselves are afflicted by such vicissitudes, such personal misfortune and suffering, as is the genesis of their own pathei-mathos.

Thus, and for example, in Europe there is the specific pathei-mathos that the First and the Second World Wars wrought. A collective learning regarding the destruction, the suffering, the brutality, the horror, of wars where wrakeful machines and mass manufactured weapons played a significant role.

All this, while sad, is perhaps the result of our basic human nature; for we are jumelle, and not only because we are "deathful of body yet deathless the inner mortal" [4] but also because it seems to me that what is good and bad resides in us all [5], nascent or alive or as part of our personal past, and that it is just so easy, so tempting, so enjoyable, sometimes, to indulge in, to do, what is bad, and often harder for us to do what is right. Furthermore, we do seem to have a tendency - or perhaps a need - to ascribe what is bad to being 'out there', in something abstract or in others while neglecting or not perceiving our own faults and mistakes and while asserting or believing that we, and those similar to us or who we are in agreement with, are right and thus have the 'correct', the righteous, answers. Thus it is often easier to find what is bad 'out there' rather than within ourselves; easier to hate than to love, especially as a hatred of impersonal others sometimes affords us a reassuring sense of identity and a sense of being 'better' than those others.

Will it therefore require another thousand, or two thousand, or three thousand years - or more or less millennia - before we human beings en masse, world-wide, are empathic, tolerant, kind, and honourable? Is such a basic change in our nature even possible? Certainly there are some - and not only ideologues of one kind or another - who would argue and who have argued that such a change is not desirable. And is such a change in our nature contingent, as I incline to believe, upon the fair allocation of world resources and solving problems such as hunger and poverty and preventing preventable diseases? Furthermore, how can or could or should such a basic change be brought about - through an organized religion or religions, or through individual governments and their laws and their social and political and economic and educational policies, or through a collocation of governments, world-wide; or through individuals reforming themselves and personally educating others by means of, for example, the common culture of pathei-mathos which all humans share and which all human societies have contributed to for thousands of years? Which leads us on to questions regarding dogma, faith, and dissent; and to questions regarding government and compulsion and 'crime and punishment' and whether or not 'the needs of the many outweigh the needs of the few'; and also to questions regarding the efficacy of the reforming, spiritual, personal way given that spiritual ways teaching love, tolerance, humility, and compassion - and virtuous as they are, and alleviating and preventing suffering as they surely have - have not after several thousand years effected such a change in humans en masse.

I have to admit that I have no definitive or satisfactory answers to all these, and similar, questions; although my own pathei-mathos - and my lamentable four-decade long experience as an extremist, an ideologue, and as a selfish opinionated inconsiderate person - incline me to prefer the reforming, spiritual, personal way since I feel that such an approach, involving as it does a personal study of, a personal transmission of, the culture of pathei-mathos - and a personal knowing and a living of the humility that the culture of pathei-mathos teaches - is a way that does not cause nor contribute to the suffering that still so blights this world. A personal preference for such a numinous way even though I am aware of three things: of my past propensity to be wrong and thus of the necessary fallible nature of my answers; of the limited nature and thus the long time-scale (of many millennia) that such a way implies; and that it is possible, albeit improbable except in Science Fiction, that good people of honourable intentions may some day find a non-suffering-causing way by which governments or society or perhaps some new form of governance may in some manner bring about that change, en masse, in our human nature required to evolve us into individuals of empathy, compassion, and honour, who thus have something akin to a 'prime directive' to guide them in their dealings with those who are different, in whatever way, from ourselves.

Were I to daydream about some future time when such a galactic 'prime directive' exists, directing we spacefaring humans not to interfere in the internal affairs of non-terrans who are different, in whatever way, from ourselves, then I would be inclined to speculate that unless we by then have fundamentally and irretrievably changed ourselves for the better then it would not be long before some human or some human authority, somewhere, manufactured some sly excuse to order to try and justify ignoring it. For that is what we have done, among ourselves, for thousands of years; making then breaking some treaty or other; making some excuse to plunder resources; having some legal institution change some existing law or make some new law to give us the 'right' to do what it is we want to do; or manufacture some new legislative or governing body in order to 'legalize' what we do or have already done. Always using a plethora of words - and, latterly, legalese - to persuade others, and often ourselves, that what we do or are about to do or have already done is justified, justifiable, necessary, or right.

Perhaps the future excuse to so interfere contrary to a prime directive would be the familiar one of 'our security'; perhaps it would be an economic one of needing to exploit 'their' resources; perhaps it would be one regarding the threat of 'terrorism'; perhaps it would be the ancient human one, hallowed by so much blood, of 'our' assumed superiority, of 'their system' being 'repressive' or 'undemocratic' or of they - those 'others' - being 'backward' or 'uncivilized' and in need of being enlightened and 're-educated' by our 'progressive' ideas. Or, more probable, it would be some new standard or some new fashionable political or social or even religious dogma by which we commend ourselves on our progress and which we use, consciously or otherwise, to judge others by.

The current reality is that even if we had or soon established a terran 'prime directive' directing we humans not to interfere in the internal affairs of other humans here on Earth who are different, in whatever way, from ourselves, it is fairly certain it "would not be long before some human or some human authority, somewhere, manufactured some sly excuse to order to try and justify ignoring it..."

Which mention of a terran 'prime directive' leads to two of the other questions which cause me to vacillate between optimism and pessimism in regard to our future as a species. The question of increasing population, and the question of the finite resources of this Earth. Which suggests to me, as some others, that - especially as the majority of people now live in urban areas - a noble option is for us, as a species, to cooperate and betake ourselves to colonize our Moon, then Mars, and seek to develope such technology as would take us beyond our Solar System. For if we do not do this then the result would most probably be, at some future time, increasing conflict over land and resources, mass migrations (probably resulting in more conflict) and such governments or authorities as then exist forced by economic circumstance to adopt policies to reduce or limit their own population. Global problems probably exasperated still further by the detrimental changes that available evidence indicates could possibly result from what has been termed 'climate change' [6].

But is the beginning of this noble option of space colonization viable in the near future? Possibly not, given that the few countries that have the resources, the space expertise and the technology necessary - and the means to develop existing space technology - do not consider such exploration and colonization as a priority, existing as they seem to do in a world where nation-States still compete for influence and power and where conflict - armed, deadly, and otherwise - is still regarded as a viable solution to problems.

Which leads we human beings, with our jumelle character, confined to this small planet we call Earth, possibly continuing as we have, for millennia, continued: a quarrelsome species, often engaged (like primates) in minor territorial disputes; in our majority unempathic; often inconsiderate, often prejudiced (even though we like to believe otherwise); often inclined to place our self-interest and our pleasure first; often prone to being manipulated or to manipulating others; often addicted to the slyness of words spoken and written and heard and read; often believing 'we' are better than 'them'; and fighting, raping, hating, killing, invading here, interfering there. And beset by the problems wrought by increasing population, by dwindling resources, by mass migrations, by continuing armed conflicts (regional, local, supranational, over some-thing) and possibly also affected by the effects of climate change.

Yet also, sometimes despite ourselves, we are beings capable of - and have shown over millennia - compassion, kindness, gentleness, tolerance, love, fairness, reason, and a valourous self-sacrifice that is and has been inspirational. But perhaps above all we have, in our majority, exuded and kept and replenished the virtue of hope; hoping, dreaming, of better times, a better future, sometime, somewhere - and not, as it happens, for ourselves but for our children and their children and the future generations yet to be born. And it is this hope that changes us, and has changed us, for the better, as our human culture of pathei-mathos so eloquently, so numinously, and so tragically, reveals.

Thus the question seems to be whether we still have hope enough, dreams enough, nobility enough, and can find some way to change ourselves, to thus bring a better - a more fairer, more just, more compassionate - future into-being without causing or contributing to the suffering which so blights, and which has so blighted, our existence on Earth.

Personally, I am inclined to wonder if the way we need - the hope, the dream, we need - is that of setting forth to explore and colonize our Moon, then Mars, and then the worlds beyond our Solar System, guided by a prime directive.

∘∘∘

Notes

[1] I understand 'the good' as what alleviates or does not cause suffering; what is compassionate; what is honourable; what is reasoned and balanced. Honour being here, and elsewhere in my recent writings, understood as the instinct for and an adherence to what is fair, dignified, and valourous.

[2] I have expanded, a little, on what I mean by 'the culture of pathei-mathos' in my tract *Questions of Good, Evil, Honour, and God.*

[3] As defined by my 'philosophy of pathei-mathos', I understand innocence as "an attribute of those who, being personally unknown to us, are therefore unjudged us by and who thus are given the benefit of the doubt. For this presumption of innocence of others – until direct personal experience, and individual and empathic knowing of them, prove otherwise – is the fair, the reasoned, the numinous, the human, thing to do. Empathy and πάθει μάθος incline us toward treating other human beings as we ourselves would wish to be treated; that is they incline us toward fairness, toward self-restraint, toward being well-mannered, and toward an appreciation and understanding of innocence."

[4] Pœmandres (Corpus Hermeticum), 15 - διὰ τοῦτο παρὰ πάντα τὰ ἐπὶ γῆς ζῷα διπλοῦς ἐστιν ὁ ἄνθρωπος

As I noted in my translation of and commentary on the Pœmandres tract, "Jumelle. For διπλοῦς. The much underused and descriptive English word jumelle - from the Latin gemellus - describes some-thing made in, or composed of, two parts, and is therefore most suitable here, more so than common words such as 'double' or twofold."

[5] qv. Sophocles, Antigone, v.334, vv.365-366

> πολλὰ τὰ δεινὰ κοὐδὲν ἀνθρώπου δεινότερον πέλει...
> σοφόν τι τὸ μηχανόεν τέχνας ὑπὲρ ἐλπίδ᾽ ἔχων
> τοτὲ μὲν κακόν, ἄλλοτ᾽ ἐπ᾽ ἐσθλὸν ἕρπει

> There exists much that is strange, yet nothing
> Has more strangeness than a human being...
> Beyond his own hopes, his cunning
> In inventive arts – he who arrives

[6] Many people have a view about 'climate change' - for or against - for a variety of reasons. My own view is that the scientific evidence available at the moment seems to indicate that there is a change resulting from human activity and that this change could possibility be detrimental, in certain ways, to us and to the other life with which we share this planet. The expressions 'seems to indicate' and 'could possibly be' are necessary given that this view of mine might need to be, and should be, reassessed if and when new evidence or facts become available.

Bibliography

° W. Bright. *The Gospel Of John. In West-Saxon*. Heath & Co., London. 1906.

° D. Myatt. *Corpus Hermeticum: Eight Tractates*. Translations And Commentaries. CreateSpace. 2017

° D. Myatt. *Classical Paganism And The Christian Ethos*. CreateSpace. 2017

° D. Myatt. *The Gospel According to John*. Translation And Commentary. Volume I. Chapters 1 - 4. CreateSpace. 2017

° Nestle-Aland. *Novum Testamentum Graece*, 28th revised edition. Deutsche Bibelgesellschaft, Stuttgart. 2012

° A.D. Nock & A-J. Festugiere, *Corpus Hermeticum*, Paris, 1972

° R.A. Reitzenstein. *Die hellenistischen Mysterienreligionen*. Teubner, Leipzig, 1927.